THE CONSTELLATION LEO

AMY C. REA

childsworld.com

Published by The Child's World®
800-599-READ • www.childsworld.com

Photography Credits
Photographs ©: Shutterstock Images, cover (illustration), cover (background), 1 (illustration), 1 (background), 2 (illustration), 2–3, 5, 6, 9 (illustration), 14 (Hercules), 14 (background), 18, 21; E. Slawik/NSF/AURA/M. Zamani/NOIRLab, cover (constellation), 1 (constellation), 2 (constellation), 9 (constellation), 25; Johannes Hevelius/Barry Lawrence Ruderman Antique Maps Inc., 10; REU program/NSF/AURA/NOIRLab, 11; iStockphoto, 13; Heritage Art/Heritage Images/Hulton Archive/Getty Images, 17; Metropolitan Museum of Art, 22; Jim Cumming/Shutterstock Images, 26; A Linna/China News Service/VCG/AP Images, 27; Li San/Shutterstock Images, 29; Design elements from Shutterstock Images

ISBN Information
9781503875807 (Reinforced Library Binding)
9781503876224 (Portable Document Format)
9781503876842 (Online Multi-user eBook)
9781503877344 (Electronic Publication)

LCCN 2025938261

Printed in the United States of America

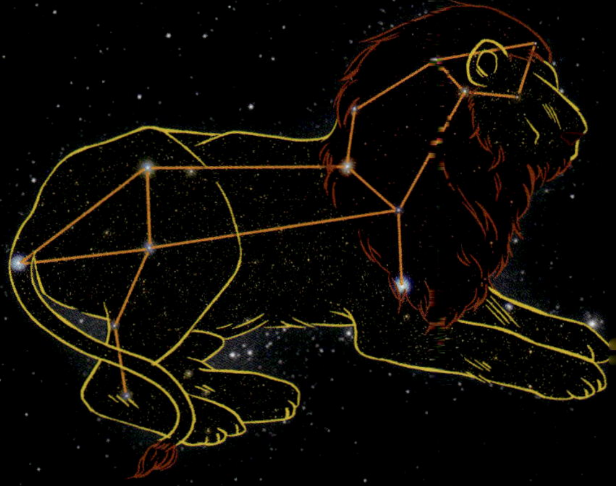

ABOUT THE AUTHOR
Amy C. Rea grew up in northern Minnesota and now lives in a Minneapolis suburb with her family. She writes frequently about traveling around Minnesota and loves spending time with her family and her silly dog.

TABLE OF CONTENTS

CHAPTER ONE

The Constellation Leo

The sky is full of stars. Stars are large balls of hot gas that shine brightly. Most are easiest to see at night. But there is one star that is easy to see in the daytime. The Sun is the closest star to Earth. It is 93 million miles (150 million km) away.

There are trillions of stars in the **universe**. Some scientists think there may be as many as one septillion stars. One septillion is the number one followed by 24 zeros. Stars appear tiny because they are so far away. But many are larger than the Sun. Some stars live for a few million years. Others live up to trillions of years.

The Sun looks larger than other stars because of how close it is to Earth.

People have noticed shapes in the stars for thousands of years.

For thousands of years, people have looked up at the stars. Some people drew imaginary lines between stars to create pictures. These pictures are called constellations. Today, **astronomers** recognize 88 official constellations. The oldest records of constellations are in cave paintings that are 30,000 years old. They show the constellations as animals, people, and objects. **Myths** about constellations exist all over the world. These myths have been found in European, African, Asian, and Native American art and stories.

Leo the Lion is the twelfth-largest constellation. It is made up of 13 stars. Its brightest star is Regulus, which is the twenty-first-brightest star in the sky. Regulus is 75 times bigger than the Sun.

Leo also has an asterism. An asterism is a pattern of stars that is not officially a constellation. Leo's asterism is called the Sickle. A sickle is a curved blade. The asterism looks like a backward question mark. It is made up of six stars. One of those stars is Regulus, Leo's brightest star. The Sickle makes up Leo's mane. Algieba (al-JEE-buh) is found where Leo's head meets the body. *Algieba* means "lion's mane." A triangle of three bright stars marks the back of Leo's body.

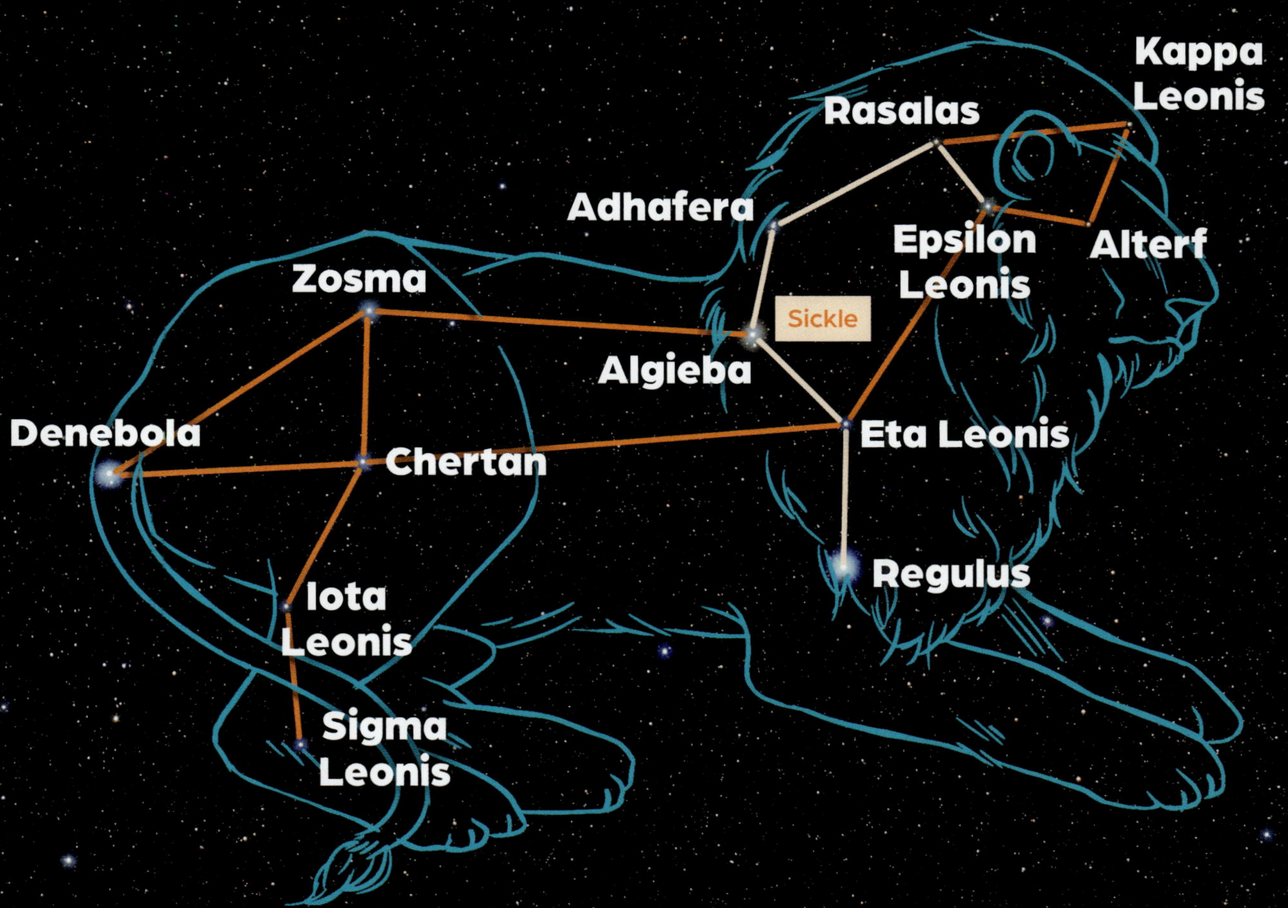

Leo is made up of 13 stars.

LEO MINOR

Leo is not the only lion in the sky. Leo Minor, the Little Lion, sits just above Leo's head. A Polish astronomer named Johannes Hevelius introduced this constellation in 1687. There are no myths associated with Leo Minor.

Johannes Hevelius published a star map with a drawing of Leo Minor.

Three galaxies make up the Leo Triplet.

Space objects near a constellation are considered part of that constellation. Many constellations have **galaxies**. Leo has many galaxies. People need medium or large telescopes to see them. Leo's galaxies include Messier 65, 66, 95, 96, and 105. Messier 65 and 66 are part of the Leo Triplet along with NGC 3628. The Leo Triplet is a small cluster of three bright galaxies.

CHAPTER TWO

THE ORIGIN OF THE MYTH

Leo is one of the oldest known constellations. **Ancient** Mesopotamians may have recognized it by 3200 BC. Babylonians called Regulus *Lugal*. This name means "king," and the star was listed as "the star in the lion's chest." Many other ancient cultures recognized Leo's stars as a lion.

Greek astronomers studied the work of other ancient astronomers. The Greco-Roman astronomer and mathematician Ptolemy (TAH-luh-mee) wrote about the constellation Leo in AD 150. Ptolemy described 48 constellations. He did not invent the constellations. But he was the first known person to write them down. Most of these constellations are included in the 88 modern constellations.

LEO AND THE ANCIENT EGYPTIANS

Ancient Egyptians believed that the constellation Leo was important to farming. Leo appeared in the hottest months of the year. The hot months were when the Nile River flooded. Farmers needed the river's water for their crops. They believed Leo was a good omen. The paths they built to help the river water reach the crops included statues of lions.

Some scholars think the Great Sphinx in Giza, Egypt, represented Leo and Virgo, another nearby constellation. Virgo is a young woman. A Sphinx has a lion's body and a human head.

Hercules has his own constellation.

The ancient Greeks told stories about gods, goddesses, and monsters. The myths were kept alive by telling the stories over and over. Even though they were not yet in books, people remembered them. Leo represents an important lion in Greek mythology. Hercules was a son of Zeus, the king of the gods. He had to battle a strong, scary lion. It was not an easy task. But Hercules succeeded. Zeus honored the battle by putting Leo into the sky as a constellation. This was a way to remember how **heroic** and brave Hercules was.

The Greeks believed that struggle and suffering could be good for a person. Hercules struggled and suffered while fighting the mighty lion. He became famous when he won.

CHAPTER THREE

THE STORY OF LEO

Hercules was a son of Zeus. His mother was a mortal woman named Alcmene (alk-MEE-nee). Zeus's jealous wife, Hera, tried to make life difficult for Hercules. When Hercules was a baby, Hera sent snakes to kill him in his cradle. But Hercules fought the snakes. They were the first of many monsters he would fight in his lifetime.

Hercules's great-grandfather was Perseus, another Greek hero. Before Hercules was born, Zeus said the next **descendant** of Perseus would rule over Greece. He thought Hercules would be born next. But Hera had other plans. Another woman was pregnant with a descendant of Perseus. Hera made sure that other baby was born first. Eurystheus (yoo-RISS-thee-yuss) became king. Hercules later became his servant. Eurystheus ordered Hercules to complete 12 difficult tasks, or labors. The labors were things most humans could not do. No one knew if Hercules could do any or all of them.

Hercules began fighting monsters almost as soon as he was born.

Some stories say Hera raised the Nemean Lion like a pet.

The first labor Eurystheus gave to Hercules was to kill a lion in the town of Nemea. The lion was eating cattle. It would kill any human that came close. But this was no ordinary lion. Its skin could not be cut with any weapon. The lion was so big and strong that killing it seemed impossible. The king ordered Hercules to bring him the lion's skin.

Hercules tracked down the lion. First, he tried hitting the lion with a bow and arrow. But the arrow bounced right off the lion's skin. Hercules knew then he would have to fight the lion with his bare hands. Luckily, Hercules was very, very strong.

The lion had gone into a cave with two entrances. Thinking quickly, Hercules blocked one of the entrances. He went through the other to find the lion. The two fought fiercely. The lion swiped its razor-sharp claws at Hercules. But it was no match for Zeus's son. Hercules wrestled the lion, strangling it. Hercules's first labor was complete!

THE 12 LABORS

Hercules had to complete 11 other tasks after slaying the Nemean Lion. The first was slaying the Hydra. Then Hercules had to capture a deer and a boar. He had to clean a king's stables in one day. The stables held more than 1,000 cattle. Hercules had to hunt man-eating birds and capture a mad bull. He had to capture man-eating horses and steal a belt from a warrior queen. Then Hercules had to take cattle from a three-headed, six-legged monster named Geryon. Next, he had to bring back golden apples from the edge of the world. Finally, Hercules had to bring Cerberus up from the underworld. This three-headed dog guarded the gates.

The Nemean Lion was no match for Hercules.

Hercules can be identified in Greek art because he is often shown wearing his lion skin. Some Greek writers said Hercules killed another lion earlier in his life, and that lion's skin is what he wore.

The hero realized the lion's special skin could protect him. Hercules cut off the skin using the lion's claws. He wore the skin around his shoulders. Then he went to prove to Eurystheus that he had killed the lion. The king was impressed. But he was also scared of what Hercules could do. Eurystheus told Hercules not to come through the gates of the city. He sent instructions for the remaining labors through a messenger. Zeus wanted to honor his son's victory. He placed the lion into the night sky as the constellation Leo.

CHAPTER FOUR

The Myth of Leo in Other Cultures

Many cultures saw Leo as a lion. But they told different stories about the lion. The Roman poet Ovid wrote a myth about a young man named Pyramus (PEER-ih-muss) and a young woman named Thisbe (THIHZ-bee). They wanted to get married. But their parents tried to keep them apart.

The couple decided to meet in secret by a mulberry bush. Thisbe arrived first. As she waited for Pyramus, a lion jumped out of the bushes and scared her away. The white veil she wore fell off as she ran. Then Pyramus arrived and found the veil. He thought the lion had killed Thisbe. He became very sad and died of sorrow. But Thisbe was not dead. She returned and found Pyramus dead. That made her sad, and she died, too. Some say the Roman god Jupiter put Thisbe's veil into the sky with the lion. The veil is now known as Coma Berenices (KOH-muh beh-ruh-NY-seez).

COMA BERENICES

Coma Berenices means "Berenice's Hair." The constellation is named after Queen Berenice II of Egypt. It is one of the few constellations named after a real person. Most are named after people in myths. For many years, this constellation was considered part of Leo's tail. But in the 1500s, it became its own constellation.

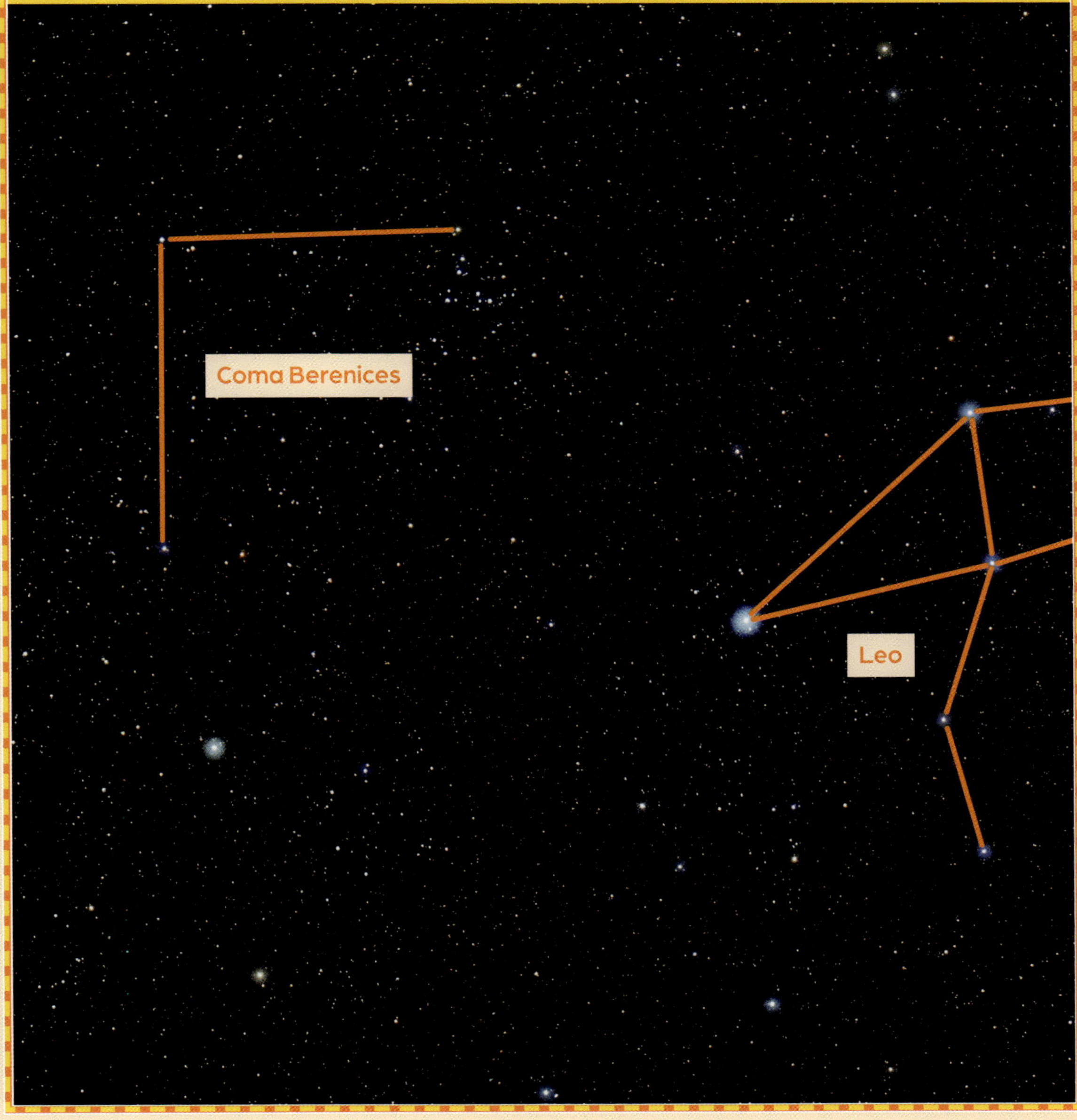

Ojibwe stargazers see a mountain lion's long tail as the Sickle of Leo.

Native American peoples recognize different constellations. Ojibwe stargazers recognize the Sickle of Leo as being part of a big cat. But they see the Sickle as the tail. *Mishi Bizhiw*, Curly Tail or the Great Panther, is made of stars from Leo and Cancer. The stars represent a mountain lion. The constellation was a sign of spring. When people saw it overhead, they knew it was no longer safe to walk on frozen rivers or lakes.

Chinese astronomers saw yet another animal in Leo's Sickle. It was part of a chain of 17 stars that made the Yellow Dragon. This constellation represented Huangdi. This ruler is said to be the founder of Chinese **civilization**.

People still honor and celebrate Huangdi.

CHAPTER FIVE

How to Find Leo in the Sky

Leo is a large constellation. It has several bright stars. That makes it easy to find without using a telescope. Some constellations can be seen only in the Northern **Hemisphere** or the Southern Hemisphere. But Leo can be seen in both. The only place Leo is not visible is in Antarctica

Leo can usually be seen in the Northern Hemisphere in the months of March, April, and May. The constellation moves west, and by the end of July it has sunk below the western **horizon**. People in the Southern Hemisphere may see it in September and October.

THE ZODIAC

Leo is one of the original 12 constellations in the zodiac. Babylonians first created the zodiac in 500 BC. The constellations in the zodiac lie along the ecliptic. This is the circular path the Sun seems to take through the constellations. Throughout the year, the Sun appears to move in front of each of these constellations. Leo's time is July 23 to August 22.

Finding the Sickle of Leo or the triangle can help people find Leo.

The best way to look for Leo in the night sky is to first find the Big Dipper. This asterism is made up of seven bright stars. It looks like a bowl with a curved handle. The side of the Big Dipper's bowl is above Leo. The two stars that make up the side of the bowl are called pointer stars. The pointer stars point down at Leo's head. To help remember how to find Leo, people might think of the Big Dipper's bowl as having holes in it. Water in the bowl drips out and lands on Leo.

GLOSSARY

ancient (AYN-shunt) Something that is ancient is very old or belongs to times long ago. Ancient Mesopotamians may have recognized Leo as early as 3200 BC.

astronomers (uh-STRAW-nuh-murz) Astronomers are scientists who study stars and other objects in space. Ptolemy studied the work of other astronomers.

boar (BOHR) A boar is a male pig. Hercules had to capture a boar as one of his labors.

civilization (si-vuh-lih-ZAY-shun) A civilization is a complex society with laws and culture. Huangdi is said to be the founder of Chinese civilization.

descendant (dih-SEN-dent) A descendant is a younger family member, such as a child, grandchild, or great-grandchild. Hercules was a descendant of Perseus.

galaxies (GAL-uhk-seez) Galaxies are groups of dust, gases, and billions of stars held together by gravity. The constellation Leo has many galaxies within it.

heroic (hih-ROH-ik) A heroic action is done with bravery and courage. Zeus celebrated Hercules's heroic defeat of the Nemean Lion.

horizon (huh-RYE-zin) The horizon is the line where the ground or water seems to meet the sky. By July and August, Leo sinks below the horizon for viewers in the Northern Hemisphere.

Hydra (HYE-druh) In Greek mythology, the Hydra is a many-headed monster, and when one of its heads is cut off, two or more heads grow back. Hercules had to slay the Hydra as the second of his 12 labors.

myths (MITHS) Myths are stories from a community of people that tell of their beliefs. The Nemean Lion is one of the myths of Leo.

universe (YOO-nih-vers) The universe is everything that exists in space. The universe is full of galaxies, stars, and other space objects.

FAST FACTS

- Constellations are groupings of stars in the sky that form pictures. Stars are glowing balls of gas throughout the universe. The Sun is a star.
- Leo is the twelfth-largest constellation. It is made up of 13 stars. The brightest star in Leo is Regulus.
- The Sickle is a famous asterism in Leo.
- Leo has been recognized for thousands of years. Many cultures have seen it as a lion.
- In Greek mythology, Leo represents the Nemean Lion. The hero Hercules battled this mighty lion.
- A Roman story says Leo is the lion from the Pyramus and Thisbe myth. Ojibwe stargazers see Leo as another big cat, a mountain lion. In Chinese astronomy, Leo is part of the Yellow Dragon.
- Leo can be seen in both the Northern and Southern Hemispheres.
- Leo can be found by locating the Big Dipper and looking below the dipper's bowl.

ONE STRIDE FURTHER

- Do you think the constellation Leo looks like a lion? Or do you see a different shape in its stars?
- This book discussed several myths about Leo. Which was your favorite and why? Where could you go to learn more about your favorite story?
- Have you ever found Leo in the night sky? What about other constellations? Do you have a favorite constellation?

FIND OUT MORE

IN THE LIBRARY

Read, John A. *A Kid's Guide to the Night Sky.* Naperville, IL: Sourcebooks, 2024.

Van De Car, Nikki. *The Junior Astrologer's Handbook: A Kid's Guide to Astrological Signs, the Zodiac, and More*. Philadelphia, PA: Running Press Kids, 2021.

Wilson, Sierra. *The Constellation Aquarius*. Parker, CO: The Child's World, 2026.

ON THE WEB

Visit our website for links about Leo:

childsworld.com/links

Note to Parents, Caregivers, Teachers, and Librarians: We routinely verify our web links to make sure they are safe and active sites. So encourage your readers to check them out!

INDEX